T0354997

I Was Number 13

I Was Number 13

JACK DOUGLAS DAVIDSON

I WAS NUMBER 13

iUniverse books may be ordered through booksellers or by contacting:

iUniverse
1663 Liberty Drive
Bloomington, IN 47403
www.iuniverse.com
844-349-9409

Because of the dynamic nature of the Internet, any web addresses or links contained in this book may have changed since publication and may no longer be valid. The views expressed in this work are solely those of the author and do not necessarily reflect the views of the publisher, and the publisher hereby disclaims any responsibility for them.

Any people depicted in stock imagery provided by Getty Images are models, and such images are being used for illustrative purposes only.
Certain stock imagery © Getty Images.

ISBN: 978-1-6632-7115-0 (sc)
ISBN: 978-1-6632-7117-4 (hc)
ISBN: 978-1-6632-7116-7 (e)

Library of Congress Control Number: 2025902976

Print information available on the last page.

iUniverse rev. date: 02/14/2025

FOREWORD

by Jim Baynham

Jack Davidson lives with his wife, Jo, in the retirement center called Brookdale Cub Hill in Garland, Texas. They are both very active in contributing their skills toward making the residents lives meaningful and enjoyable. His life stories are both honest and insightful and may show an inquiring senior in any situation how one man has coped successfully with the trials and opportunities during his lifetime. I have worked with writers as they told their stories here at Brookdale Club Hill and present Jack's work as an excellent example of the clear messages we all wish to leave as our contribution to our heir's knowledge of what it took to complete our life's journey.

WHAT WAS YOUR DAD LIKE WHEN YOU WERE A CHILD?

My Dad was a very intelligent, community-minded farmer with many other skills and talents. He was quite an inventor even though his academic education was limited. (Less than high school graduation). H read newspapers, magazines and books often. In that way he was very self-educated.

Sadly, my Dad also had a horrible temper! For example, I have been in a nice Packard automobile with him when he zoomed across a rough grass pasture and intentionally hit a cow that had defied his herding directions. The action broke the cow's leg. Eventually, the cow had to be disposed of because we could not set her leg well enough to prevent her standing on it and cause the bandages to come off.

Unfortunately, my Dad's temper was "fired" toward his children on some occasions. Mostly, I was very afraid of him and spoke only when he spoke to me and asked a question. On one occasion I was moving a plow from one field to the next when a tire slipped off at a pipe culvert and bent an irrigation pipe because the steel culvert pipe was a tiny bit too short for the width of the plow. I immediately told Dad about the incident when I arrived at the field where he was. I was very worried about what he would do. Instead, he just made an ugly face and walked away. I was very relieved.

Dad had served as school trustee in our rural school district. He also got elected as Precinct 4 County Commissioner in Moore County, Texas, where we lived. He served for twelve years and never lost an election. Because I took typing in high school and owned a little portable typewriter, I typed many campaign letters for Dad's elections.

Dad was very active in our little community Methodist Church. He gave generously so that we could at least have a part-time minister. Also, he donated all of the materials and part of the labor for a church parsonage when the church finally got enough to pay a full-time minister.

In additional to our 480-acre farm in Moore County, Texas, my Dad purchased a 5,000 –acre ranch near Walsenburg, Colorado in the 1950's. Sadly, a drought hit both the farm and the ranch soon after he bought the ranch. Because he was very leveraged at the banks for his livestock, he was forced to sell about all his cows and sheep to pay off loans. With no way of generating cash through either farming or ranching, Dad was forced to trade the Colorado ranch for a very old multi-story building in downtown Amarillo, Texas. Since he was retired from the farm he simply operated a furniture store and a parking lot in that building in order to generate some income.

Dad had many skills in addition to being an excellent farmer. For example he could build a complete house from scratch. He also purchased old World War II military barracks from a nearby army base and converted them into apartment buildings. He also frequently bought property on main street in small towns and later sold the best part to oil companies for new gasoline service stations or sold them to fast food companies. Later he would sell the remainder of the property at a full profit.

For most of his children, Dad furnished money for a college education. We worked at many jobs, ran a rural paper route and even sold our blood to gain enough money to pay tuition and buy books.

In a nutshell, my Dad was a warm and wonderful man with a severe personality characteristic of a big temper. In his elder days, however, the "teddy bear" inside this tough guy came out. We enjoyed many conversations in person and on the phone in his last few years. During those years he was writing and recording religious hymns.

WHAT WAS YOUR MOM LIKE WHEN YOU WERE A CHILD?

My Mom, Daisy Lela (Baker) Davidson was a "country girl" in every sense. She was full of love but she could become quite frustrated with a stubborn animal and really become rather violent with them. She knew and used many of them of the ancient methods such as lye soap manufacturing. During the fall of the year we always butchered several hogs so that we would have ham, bacon, sausage, etc. during the winter.

It was my job to take the slabs of hog fat and slice it into little squares. We then cooked those squares of hog fat in a large black cooking pot outside over a natural gas flame. The process was known as "rendering the lard" from the hog. The little squares were left with only a shell which we removed from the pot of lard (grease) and dried. The squares were then known as "cracklings". They were then used to put into homemade corn bread. My Mother called it "crackling cornbread." It was delicious!

Mom was very strict with her children. (This DID NOT apply to her grandchildren! She had borne 13 and lost two to miscarriage. To say that she was somewhat of a fanatic would be an understatement. For example, once she whipped me with a belt because I had used the word "gosh" in a sentence. Another time, she whipped me with a belt after I came back from a walk toward the dry lake bed on the neighbor's property. I had no idea why I was being whipped until I learned that my brothers had gone hunting on that property and I was not invited (I was too young), so I simply waited a while and then followed them. I was being disciplined because of the potential danger of being accidentally shot.

By the time I was born (I was her thirteenth and last child) Mom had become a very devout "Pentecostal" Christian. There was many, many "don'ts" within that religion. Also, we attended MANY services. We attended "her church" twice on Sunday, once on Wednesday and Friday nights and every weekday night when there was a "revival" going on. Since we could not attend movies, go dancing or mix with other teens at school entertainment events. During teen years, we were somewhat "outcasts" within our school. For example, on prom nights, we could only watch school-provided 16mm movies in the auditorium instead of going to an actual dance. We WERE allowed to be in the high school band. So we learned to march some of my siblings learned to play their instruments rather well. I carried a bass clef baritone brass instrument, but we were having a drought (lack of rain) on the farm, so Dad could not afford for me to ever take lessons on how to actually play that baritone. However,

I really worked on doing a good job of marching during football game half-time shows.

Interestingly, while Mom was not a great cook, each of her daughters (three of four lived to adulthood) were excellent cooks! Mom could cook about any kind of meat, pinto beans and mashed potatoes. She also make and bake wonderful yeast rolls and yeast bread loaves. After we finally got electricity at the farm and Mom got a freezer, she was excited to buy "store bought" sliced load bread and place it in the freezer. No longer did we have home made rolls or loaf bread.

Mom was quite the gardener! We had very old existing annuals such as grapes and rhubarb. We planted black-eyed peas, onions, corn, English Peas, and carrots almost every year. We also usually grew okra and had a few tomato plants. We fertilized the garden with Vigaro and with manure from the chicken houses.

Speaking of chickens, Mom purchased up to 100 baby chicks in the early spring. The rural mail carrier brought the boxes of baby chicks and would stop at our Mailbox ¼ mile from our home and honk the horn on her vehicle until got someone's attention. She made certain that the baby chicks were not left out in the weather very long. We got the boxes of chicks and treated each chicken with a purple liquid which I suppose was an antibiotic and then placed them under a warm reflective heater known as a "brooder". We made certain that the chicks always had water and food.

When the chicks became "pullets", we butchered them and took them to Dumas, a nearby town, and sold them. This was one way that Mom generated a bit of personal income. Another way was taking fresh milk to town and selling it by the gallon and by taking large cans of cream to the railroad station at Channing, Texas, and sending it to the creamery in Amarillo, Texas on the train. A few days later Mom would receive a little check in the mail and her metal cream cans would be sent back to Channing where we would drive over and pick them up. I loved watching the railroad telegraphers using the Morse Code Keys to send messages either related to the railroad or Western Union telegraph. Also, sometimes the steam locomotives would rush through the station without stopping, but the U.S. Mail would be retrieved from the cab of the locomotive with a long metal hook. They rarely missed it or dropped the mail. To this day I love seeing steam locomotives.

Mom was very good at raising a little cash to spend on groceries and animal feed. The feed would be in cotton sacks which had a nice design printed on them. For most of my early years, the only shirts that I had were "manufactured" on Mom's old treadle-type Singer Sewing Machine. She was a proficient seamstress and made most of the boys' shirts and the girls' dresses.

WHAT WERE YOUR GRANDPARENTS LIKE?

Sadly, I never saw or had any contact with any of my grandparents. Both my Father and my Mother were the youngest of very large families and I was the youngest of their 13 children. On both Mom's side and Dad's side, my grandparents passed away many years before I was born. In Dad's case, his Father passed away when Dad was only 14 years of age. Dad was 40 years of age when I was born.

WHAT GAMES DID YOU PLAY OR WHAT DID YOU DO FOR FUN AS A CHILD?

I was in elementary school beginning in September of 1946. Today is August 22, 2023. Sadly, my recall is very limited for those years. I will try to give a broad description, but details would help make more sense.

At Middlewell Elementary School, a two-room school house with a total staff of two, we often had organized games. If it was bad weather outside, we used recess as a time for spelling bees or even a contest or diagramming sentences. We did not fully realize that the male teacher/principal was actually causing us to improve our academics AND having a contest of fun competition with other students as we did so. Also, sometimes we all held hands so that a device that shocked us with electric current was our bad weather past time.

Outside, we had they typical swing set, teeter-toter (we called it a "see-saw"), steel rings to pull up on with out hands and arms and other invented contest games. One such game involved choosing up sides and group one standing on a mound of dirt, called a "mountain". The group not on the mountain would call for one mountain student to come and attempt to break through the connected hands of the non-mountain group. If their run caused a break through, they selected one individual to take with them back to the mountain. If the runner did not break through, then they had to join the non-mountain group. We repeated this action until one side had all of the students.

Another game involved throwing a softball over the roof of the school and the person who caught it on the other side ran around the building and tried to evade being caught by the throwing team. I believe there was a point system to decide the winner, but my recall is hazy on that.

At home, we made most of our toys. We would make sling shots from Y-shaped peach limbs and pieces of inner rubber tubes from auto tires. We also made "Caterpillar crawler tractors" from scraps of wood. We became very good at sound effects as we moved these "big machines" on the ground.

At the farm, we had calf-riding contests and target practice with a .22 rifle or pistol. At high school age, my buddy and I would take a .22 rifle and go out Saturday night and try to reduce the jackrabbit population. The jackrabbits were not edible and destroyed many crops due to their rapid multiplication. We also would attempt to reduce that population by chasing jackrabbits with a deep and shooting them from the moving jeep with a 20-gauge shotgun.

We had other ways of entertaining ourselves as we got older. For example, we played the board games of checkers and even chess. We also learned to play dominoes and "42" with dominoes.

WHAT WAS YOUR FIRST BIG TRIP?

As the youngest child, my first real trip was with Mom and Dad Weatherford, Texas, for Memorial Day (or "Decoration Day"). I alter found out that some of my older siblings (Steve Edwin, for example) were jealous that I went on the trip while they were left at the farm.

We did only a tiny amount of travel when I was a child. However, without fail, my parents returned to their home area near Fort Worth and Weatherford, Texas once a year. That was on May 30. Or "Decoration Day," which honored those who had lost their lives in wars. It was also the day that Mom and Dad returned to their family cemetery to clear the vines and brush from the graves of their parents and other family members. That cemetery was about 5 miles northwest of the town of Weatherford, Texas and was know as "Zion Hill Cemetery". On both my Mom's side and my Father's side of the family, their parents and other relatives such as siblings were buried. At lunch time, all the families gathered for lunch that was brought by those attending.

In the earliest years, we met in the very same school house where my Mother had attended elementary school. In later years, when my wife and I attended, the community had built a nice building for community meetings. This was also the annual meeting of the Zion Hill Cemetery Association. This association finally saved enough money from donations to cause the cemetery to become a perpetual care cemetery. Zion Hill Cemetery is where my wife and I expect to be buried. We already have our head stones there. Only the death date will need to be added to the head stones after we are buried. My oldest brother (unnamed and lived only 5 days) and Cecil Baker Davidson, another brother are already buried in Zion Hill Cemetery.

During the days in the area, Mom always went to stay with her brother, Albert, and his wife, Ada. I stayed there also. Dad went to Fort Worth to see his sisters. Occasionally, Mom and I went with Dad to visit the sisters, Aunt Maude and Aunt Nora and her husband, Uncle Ben.

At Uncle Albert's place, I was allowed to draw water from the shallow water well with a long can on a rope and I first learned about china eggs that were supposed to encourage free range hens to lay their eggs in certain place. Also, Uncle Albert would let me help him feed his work horses that he used to plow gardens in the Weatherford area.

There was little to do at Aunt Nora's house except be amazed by the very old telephone and its party line. I did notice that Aunt Nora was a licensed Notary Public. Many, many years later, I became a Notary Public and was licensed for many years. Sometimes, Uncle Ben would give me some attention and entertain me with magic tricks. Mostly, I just kept quiet and spoke when spoken to. The trip was not nearly "exciting" as some of my siblings supposed.

I managed to get into poison ivy and fire aunts while at Uncle Albert's house. Neither experiences were very pleasant.

How did you get
your first job?

My actual "first job" was on my father's farm and ranch. I suppose it is accurate to say that I was born into that job. On the homestead, every member of the family had responsibility at a very early age. It did not end until you left homestead. I carried "slop" to the hogs, milked cows, put out hay for feedlot calves and drove various tractors as I became older. I began to drive the Jeep four-wheel utility vehicle before I was 11 years old. Age 11 was the age when I was "granted the privilege" of driving a tractor in the field (no matter how remote) for a full 12-hour shift on Saturdays during the school year and six days a week during the summer breaks. We had tractors that were fueled by gasoline and others fueled by butane that were wheel tractors. We also had one tractor that ran on steel tracks and it was fueled by diesel. I could drive them all. Also, I obtained my Texas driver's License at age 14. Thus, during the harvest time, I began to drive both pick-up trucks and large "bobtail" grain trucks to Dumas to the Co-op Grain Elevator.

My first job off the farm was in Dumas, Texas, at a little "Mom & Pop" grocery store. This job was obtained though a high school vocational course named, "Distributive Education." My salary was $0.45 per hour. On weekdays, I worked approximately 4 hours. On Saturday, I worked for 13 hours.

That was followed by a job offered by my brother, Cecil Davidson, at $1.00 per hour. He owned a plumbing and electrical store and service in Dumas, Texas. I worked as both a plumber's apprentice and as a clerk in the supply business.

I had MANY part-time jobs during my college days at Texas A&M in College Station, Texas. These jobs included paper routes in the dining hall, addressing mail to schools for the Texas Forestry service (Smoky Bear posters, mostly), apprentice in a commercial printing shop and errand boy for my owner of a residential room that I rented. I also, worked for the local office of the United States Agriculture Department and for the Texas A&M Social Services Department.

My first job after graduating from college was in Houston, Texas, with the "Rein Company". They manufactured and sold continuous form computer paper and multi-part snap out business forms. I was in the Sales Department. I obtained the job by interviewing based on classified ads in one of the local newspapers in Houston.

___

AS A CHILD, WERE YOU
CLOSER TO YOUR FATHER
OR YOUR MOTHER?
HOW ABOUT NOW?

I was the last of my mother's 13 children. The next oldest sibling was four years older. Therefore, I spent far more time with my mother than with my father. Through high school, I mostly thought of my father as "boss". There was not a great deal of interaction after I became six years old and older. Truthfully, I was quite afraid of my father.

Gradually, as years passed my father showed his "Softer" side and I was not often the target of his incredible temper. After he reached about 65, a couple of siblings and I worked with him on his farm to attempt to save his finances. We became closer and I learned that his previous "gruff" appearance mellowed a lot. My mother, on the other hand became more wrapped up in her grandchildren and paid little attention to me or many of her other children even when we were together on holidays.

The transition of being closer to my father than to my mother was surprising. Perhaps that is common. I simply do not know.

WERE YOUR PARENTS HAPPY?

That is an interesting question: "Were your parents happy?" How does a child truly KNOW whether his or her parents are happy? Overall, I am guessing that my parents were happy and for many reasons. First, they undoubtedly loved each other very much. Secondly, they had thirteen children (Nine boys and four girls) with each other. They loved their children very much. However, they lost three children to death very early. Certainly, my Mom NEVER forgot. Their first child lived only five days and died as a baby. My Mother felt that was a "payback" because Mom and Dad got married so young and they eloped.

Although, the first baby's grave at Zion Hill Cemetery in Parker County, Texas had no gravestone until the death of both Mom and Dad, there was a little scrap of marble stone that "marked" the grave. Each year, on "Decoration Day" (May 30) when we cleaned the graves, Mom would always find that little scrap of marble and grieve over the loss of that first boy baby.

Years after the death of both Mom and Dad, I, Jack Davidson, researched the Parker County records AND the records of the funeral home that conducted the services and found two facts. First, Dad's brother, Arthur Davidson, had buried an unnamed baby in that very spot a few years before Mom and Dad's baby was buried there. I confirmed that neither baby was named.

My wife, Jo and I, purchased a gravestone honoring both sets of parents and their babies. We had the stone properly set in the exact spot where Jo found the little scrap of marble.

Further regarding the relationship between my Mom and Dad, here are some more facts. My Father had a very, very bad "temper" along with a rather "colorful" vocabulary when he was angry. (Translated, he tended to cuss a lot!) Sometimes those tantrums were directed toward my Mother. She quietly just "took it" and did not seem to get very upset. She would even comfort her children when the outbursts were directed at them and sort of "explain" her husband to the fearful children.

I truly believe that my Mom knew my Father so well and also knew that his outward gruff, bear-like demeanor was simply a coverup for the "teddy bear" that existed on the inside. She loved him and he loved here. I believe they were happy with each other. They celebrated their 50th Wedding Anniversary on the very day that the first child (a son, Robert Leo Davidson) was born to Jo (my wife) in Corpus Christi, Texas. That is a great memory to this very day.

WHAT ARE SOME OF YOUR FAVORITE FAMILY TRADITIONS?

Because our family was so large, I really wonder whether we actually had FAMILY traditions. Mom & Dad had the tradition of an annual visit to the Parker County and Forth Worth, Texas area to visit with their siblings and to clean graves at the Zion Hill Cemetery in the Parker County.

It was king of a family tradition to visit Mom & Dad during the Christmas season.

HOW DID YOUR PARENTS PICK YOUR NAME?

I was told that neither of my parents picked my name. Of my mother's 13 children, I, the last, was the ONLY child of hers that was born in a hospital. (Northwest Texas Hospital in Amarillo, Texas, USA)

Mother was so thrilled and grateful for the close and pleasant care that the nurse gave her, she told the nurse, "You name this child in honor of the wonderful care you gave me."

The nurse reportedly chose between "Frank Douglas" and "Jack Douglas". She finally decided on "Jack Douglas Davidson". That is what is on my birth certificate.

When our children were born, the first was a son. We wished to honor both grandfathers when selecting his name. My father's name was "Robert Barney" and his maternal grandfather's name was "Sardie Leo". We rejected both "Barney and "Sardie" and thus named our first child "Robert Leo Davidson".

When our second child was due, my wife was just certain that the baby was a girl. We had not selected a boy's name at all, but "Lisa Carol" was the name of the baby had been a girl.

When surprised by the appearance of a second boy, we had to hustle to find a name. We borrowed a book of names that included the supposed meaning of a name. We kind of liked one of the early entries which was "Alan". For the second name, my brother, "Cecil" had been staying in our home through part of the pregnancy. That was due to a tragic family situation in his life. We looked up the name "Cecil" in the "baby name book" and it referenced that it meant aristocrat, and similar pleasant terms. We named our second son, "Cecil Alan Davidson".

WHAT IS ONE OF THE BEST TRIPS YOU'VE EVER TAKEN? WHAT MADE IT GREAT?

My wife, Jo, and I took a trip to Williamsburg, Virginia while we were still mostly mobile. It was full of history and incredible interest. Side trips included Youngstown and Old Colonial Williamsburg.

How would you describe your childhood bedroom?

I was the thirteenth and last child born in my family. It is actually sort of funny to ask me about MY bedroom! During the winter we slept many male children together in a large bedroom. In the summer, when we hired outside people to help with the harvest, we moved outside. That was real fun when a summer storm brought rain during the middle of the night. Then, we simply moved into the house and slept on pallets of quilts over a hardwood floor.

Actually, when the brother just older than I want off to college, I did sort of have my own bedroom. BY that time my father had added an upper floor to our home. "My" bedroom was upstairs where two additional bedrooms had been added to the home. It had linoleum on the floor and a very old twin bed with a lot of very heavy home made quilts.

The reason for the heavy quilts was the fact that the only heat in the home was from natural gas heaters. The gas came from our well that was located on the farm property. In the winter, the condensed water that formed in the gas line to the home had a habit of freezing and blocking the gas. That would, of course, stop the flow of the gas to the heaters. Later, perhaps the line would thaw out the gas would flow. The problem was that there were no ignited pilot lights that could re-light the heaters. So ... each night ALL heaters were turned OFF.

We lived in the Texas Panhandle at an elevation of more than 3,000 feet above sea level. That meant that the winters got mighty cold. Often when I got up the next morning to light the heater in my bedroom there would be a fairly thick layer of ice INSIDE the windows. Brrrr. It was cold! Of course, because of the very heavy quilts I was warm while in bed. The worst part was when the gas line was still frozen and there was no gas flow to light!!!!

WHO WAS YOUR FAVORITE HIGH SCHOOL TEACHER? WHY?

I attended elementary school in a rural two-room school known as Middlewell School. (Yes, that is the correct spelling for "Middlewell". There were eight grades there taught by a man and wife.

After graduating from Middlewell Elementary, we were bussed 15 miles to the Dumas (population about 2,000) Junior High School for our 9th grade year. My favorite teacher there was "Mrs. Moser" (We NEVER knew the first names of teachers) who taught freshman (9th grade) English. Unlike many teachers in the Dumas Independent School District, Mrs. Moser seemed to express genuine caring for each of her students. The "huge" school (compared to what I had experienced) kind of caused me get lost in the shuffle. Mrs. Moser was a great teacher AND she seemed to take a personal interest in each student and, especially, those of us who came from rural areas.

Later, I had her husband, Mr. Moser, for history. He was the opposite and frequently reminded me that my older brother, Ivan, ("Rusty") was a far better student than I am.

Jack Davidson 01/29/2024

DID YOU HAVE ANY
NICKNAMES WHEN YOU
WERE A CHILD? HOW DID
YOU FEEL ABOUT THEM?

Wow! Did I have nicknames as a small child? YES!!! And I believe that each one came from my father. One of his favorite nicknames for me was, "Fuzzpot". I am not certain where on earth that came from. Another nickname that I probably earned was "Sambo". Now I suppose that there are those who might try to make something racial out of that. To the best of my knowledge nothing could be further from the truth. Instead, we had ONE black Aberdeen Angus mother cow in our herd and, obviously, she had a completely black calf. I always made pets out of almost all of our animals, but was especially fond of this gorgeous little black calf. My father decided that was sufficient reason to begin calling me "Sambo". Now, again, some would say that he meant it in a human racial way. If you knew my father you would never say that. He fully believed that all humans were God's creation and equal in every way. It is more likely that he got the name from the famous radio program, "Amos and Andy".

We regularly listened to that comedy radio program and ALL of the actors were just terrific. It was a mixture of black and white radio personalities.

By the way, we did not have electrical power service in our home at that time. The radio ran on six-volt automobile batteries. We were only were using somewhat defective batteries after they were unreliable for autos so the radio often faded during the height of the show that we were listening to. The next day we would take the battery out to the 6-volt wind charger. If the wind blew, that battery was re-charged.

Jack D Davidson 2/12/2024

Do you have a family member you wish you'd gotten to know better?

I was the last of 13 children. There was a large difference between my age and some of the older siblings. One of the older siblings that I had little contact with, but always admired was James Alfred Davidson. He adopted the nickname of "Jim" and most siblings and friends spoke to him by that name. However, several of us who had little contact with him called him "Alfred". Alfred was quite a rebel in our family. For example, when none of us before or after Jim (or Alfred) were allowed to play sports in high school, he somehow did play basketball for Dumas High School.

Also, because we were farmers, even the males in our family were usually allowed to stay on the farm rather than enter into the military service during World war II. Jim, however, chose to go to Lubbock, Texas, and volunteer for the Amy Air Corps.

Out Father was a member of the Draft Board in Moore County, Texas where we resided. Each count had a quota to meet each month for providing soldiers. The officials at the Moore County Draft Board asked Jim if it was okay that they counted his volunteering in Lubbock County to count as a fulfillment of one requirement for the quota in Moore County. Jim agreed.

Therefore, when our Father went to the monthly draft board meeting, he was surprised when his son, James Alfred Davidson, showed up on the list of soldiers satisfying that month's quota. I never knew if there was a "discussion" between our Father and Jim about the surprise.

Nevertheless, Jim served in the Army Air Corps (later, the U.S. Air Force) and was trained as a bombardier. Because he was young at the beginning of WW II, he never saw overseas duty. The war was over before he finished his training in New Mexico.

To this day, I can graphically recall the day my mother opened the letter from him stating that he was being discharged. It was handwritten on distinctive pinkish recycled paper that was the only kind available to both soldiers and civilians during that period.

Even though I was a very young child I recall Mother crying and shouting as she read Jim's words regarding his discharge. It was in the living room of our farmhouse and I did not initially know if those were tears of grief or tears of relief and happiness.

Jim used his G.I. benefits to go to Michigan State University and obtain a Bachelor of Arts in Business Administration.

Another older member of the family who was drafted out of college to service in the army was Joseph ("Joe") Brian Davidson. He served in the

Army Secret Service. One of his major assignments was in Paris, Texas, at the German POW's were held. His job was to get to know the prisoners and gain intelligence from them. While he was there he learned that there was a very high-ranking German officer among the prisoners. He dutifully reported the information. After a full interrogation by the Camp Commandant, Joe was quietly and quickly transferred to East Lansing, Michigan, as a Senior R.O.T.C. Instructor for Michigan State University. The Army later allowed Joe to continue his college education AND he was eventually awarded a Doctor of Veterinary Medicine degree. He was practicing veterinarian in Michigan for many years. I did finally get to know him in later years and even helped with plans for his funeral in Garland, Texas.

Do you have any particularly vivid memories of your grandparents?

I was the thirteenth (and last) child born to my parents in 1940. Both of my parents were also the last child born in their respective families. My father was born in 1899 and was the last of 14 children. His father passed when my father was 14 years of age. My mother was the eleventh of eleven children. Mother was also born in 1899. Therefore, all of my grandparents were passed before the year in which I was born.

I never knew any of my grandparents and knew only a few aunts and uncles. I consider that a loss.

Jack D. Davidson

WHAT GAMES OR TOYS DID YOU ENJOY MOST WHEN YOU WERE YOUNG?

We lived on a wheat and grain sorghum farm in the Texas Panhandle when I was a child. We were one county south of Oklahoma and one county east of New Mexico. We had few commercially-made toys. We did have access to sawing and drilling equipment. We made sling shots from peach Y-branches and pieces of tire tube rubber. (All auto tires has rubber "inner tubes" during that time).

We made what we considered was caterpillar type tractors from wood and welding rod for exhaust pipes. We carved wooden propellers and put the propeller on a stick. We would hold them out the window of a moving auto or other vehicle and watch the propeller turn rapidly. All of these seemed like fun.

As I grew a bit older, I actually received a "NEW" red tricycle for Christmas. I loved that vehicle and rode it as many hours a day as my chores would permit.

Then, with even more age, I was allowed to shoot the family BB gun. Finally, I was taught safety and was allowed to shoot the family .22-short rifle. I shot birds and show at jack rabbits and prairie dogs. The latter two were seldom in real danger. Finally, we had a family .22-longs pistol with a 9-inch barrel and even a 20-gauge shotgun. We used it them for target practice competition and the occasional diamond-back rattle snake threat.

WHAT WERE YOUR FAVORITE SUBJECTS IN HIGH SCHOOL?

Until just not, I had never considered whether I had any favorite subject in high school. I was not a very happy child during high school years.

Especially, in the ninth grade, I suppose that my favorite teacher AND hence my favorite subject was actually English language. Mrs. Moser was a great teacher who expressed actually caring for students. She made learning English actual fun. Also, in elementary school, we diagrammed sentences (even during recess on stormy days) and had the fun of learning. Perhaps that carried forth into the 9th grade.

As a high school senior, I was challenged in Senior English with Miss Foster. She had taught MANY of my earlier siblings and was known as a very strict and difficult teacher. Also, all writing papers turned in as homework were required to be written in fountain pen. With our cheap fountain pen, that usually meant a lot of do-overs to get rid of the ink smears that often resulted from a leaky fountain pen.

Also, during my senior year, I took a vocational course known as "Vocational Education". (Perhaps that was the foundation for my life-time interest in the world of business administration). The course requirements included going to an actual part-time local job. My very first off-farm job was in a Mom & Pop grocery store in Dumas, Texas. My pay was 45 cents per hour. It was hard work. Them for the second semester, my brother Cecil, offered me a job in his plumbing and electric supply. The pay was a lot better at $1 per hour. Also, I worked there with his son, Roger, who was only 4 years younger than me.

During my junior year in high school, my LEAST-favorite subject was American History. It was taught by Mr. Moser. He was married to my favorite teacher in the 9th grade. Mr. Moser frequently noted that my brother, Ivan, had been a far better student that I was. While that was true, it did not make me love Mr. Moser's subject matter.

HOW WOULD YOU DESCRIBE THE NEIGHBORHOOD WHERE YOU GREW UP?

I grew up in a very sparsely populated rural farming community. Our nearest neighbor was about 3 miles. That was a ranch headquarters for a very wealthy neighbor. Therefore, we had very little contact with that neighbor. We had no utility-provided electrical power and never had a telephone at our home.

In general, the neighbors were friendly and helpful. The exception was the ranch headquarters folks. Many neighbors attended a neighborhood Methodist Church on Sunday. Most of the children either attended elementary school in the local 2-room school or the "city" (about 2,000 population) high school in Dumas. Dumas was located about 15 miles from our farm and bus service was provided to both schools.

Mostly, the neighborhood was middle to lower income. The area was very drought-prone, so farming income was limited.

DID YOU HAVE A CAR IN HIGH SCHOOL OR COLLEGE?

I came from a large family. Neither I, not any of my siblings, had a car during high school. If they had a car during college it was because they personally purchased that car.

Because my brother Ivan (or "Rusty") had a 85-mile rural paper route during college, we did join to purchase a very used Plymouth auto after my freshman year in college. On Sundays, we used that auto to run the rural paper route.

Many times, we came to a creek crossing that was overrun with flooding. Often, there was a farmer waiting there with his tractor. He would hook up a chain from our car to his tractor and pull us through the high water.

When my brother came close to graduation (a six-year doctor of veterinary medicine degree) he traded the Plymouth for an Oldsmobile. Finally, immediately after his graduation, he purchased a second Oldsmobile and game me the first one.

Jack D Davidson 05/13/2024

WHAT TRADITIONS DO YOU KEEP THAT ARE RELATED TO YOUR FAMILY'S HERITAGE?

I only distinctly recall two significant family traditions of my mom and dad and their immediate children. These involve the holidays of Christmas and Memorial Day.

It was a family tradition for their children to visit Mom and Dad during the Christmas time. Since Mom and Dad are now passed, that tradition has gone away. My wife and I usually visit our oldest son and his family during the Christmas holidays now.

The Memorial Day tradition was for Mom and Dad and I to visit the Zion Hill Cemetery near Weatherford, Texas each year during Memorial Day. We would clean the grave areas of both Mom's and Dad's family. Then we would attend a community luncheon in the local Community Center.

To some extent my wife and I have kept that tradition. However, the cemetery is now under perpetual care and our mobility has become limited. So our visits are infrequent.

Our joint headstone is located in the Zion Hill Cemetery on the same row as my paternal (Davidson) grandparents and uncles and aunts.

WHAT'S ONE OF THE STRANGEST THINGS YOU'VE EVER EATEN?

This is a fun question, "WHAT'S ONE OF THE STRANGEST THING YOU'VE EVER EATEN?" Years ago, when I was a traveling graphic arts supplies and equipment salesman, one of my favorite meal spots was in the south Rio Grande Valley, Harlengen, Texas. There was a combination fuel service station and café in that town run by Barney and Sally. Sally ran the café and catered to the traveling salesman. Actually, I never ordered. I just accepted whatever Sally brought out that evening. One of the more interesting meals was rattlesnake meat. It was actually quite tasty as Sally prepared it.

Routinely, when crossing the border into Mexico, we were served fried frog legs. Food was served family style and piles and piles of great tasting food was served until you could eat no more. Because a Mexican Peso cost about 8 cents in U.S. A. money at the time, it was possible to have a fine meal at low cost.

Later, I worked for Sabre Exploration. I did aerial photography and aerial remote sensing as "Director of Data Acquisition". The President of Sabre Exploration was the only son of a very wealthy oil millionaire. That son had a gourmet appetite and found many out-of-the-way restaurants and cafes which served unknown but usually great food. That is where I learned to enjoy eating snail meat and many, many other food items that I had no idea about their identification. I also ate at super-upscale restaurants that had a lot of exotic service, but sometimes really marginal to lousy food.

Jack D Davidson 06/24/2024

HOW DID YOU LEARN TO RIDE A BICYCLE?

I learned to ride a bicycle at my rural elementary school. My classmates persuaded me to get on the seat of the bicycle and told me they would push me. That is exactly what happened, but when I looked back at some point, there was nobody pushing me. I kept pedaling and finally stopped. Eureka! I guess that I knew how to ride a bicycle.

Jack D Davidson 07/15/2024

WHAT IS ONE OF THE FAVORITE MEMORIES OF YOUR FATHER?

I have MANY favorite memories of my father. It would be hard top select just ONE. One of my pleasant (and funny) memories of my father was how he would chuckle when he heard, "Getting Too Old To Cut the Mustard" sung on the radio.

DID YOU CONSIDER ANY CAREERS OTHER THAN THE ONE WHERE YOU LANDED?

Yes, I considered MANY careers and pursued several. My first year of study at Texas A&M was in the field of architecture design.

As it turned out, My employment resume' shows many different career pursuits. Immediately after undergraduate graduation, I moved to Houston with my new wife and sold computer forms and carbon snap-out forms for a medium size printing company. About a year after I started at Rein Company, I received a letter from an individual who owned a small printing job shop in College Station, Texas, where I had worked while in college there. He offered me a full partnership in his 12-year-old company. I took him up on the deal and we tripled our production and profit in the three years I was there. However, it was day and night work that was very exhausting. I accepted an offer to become a commissioned salesman for a printing equipment and supplies company in Corpus Christi, Texas, near the Atlantic coast.

With an expanding family, I needed a more reliable income than full commission sales provided. Therefore, I took a salaried sales job in Dallas, Texas. I was still selling graphic arts equipment and supplies for a family-owned company.

However, soon a large company associated with Eastman Kodak offered me a much better salary. I still was considered a graphic arts sales representative to printing and printed circuit industries. However, it was required that I work once a week inside the retail store for photographers. I had the opportunity to go to many Eastman Kodak schools and receive excellent training.

A graphic arts customer offered to double my salary at Kodak Stores. It was a new company and a high risk, but by that time we had a second boy in the family. My wife and I decided to take the risk for the additional income.

The company was involved in petroleum, hard rock mining and geothermal exploration. Most of their techniques involved airborne (fixed wing airplanes) remote sensing equipment and aerial photography. They also had an extensive graphic arts and aerial photography laboratory. *This was, by far, the most interesting and satisfying job in my entire career.* I was able to combine my graphic arts experience and photographic experience to eventually become the Director of Data Acquisition for Sabre Exploration in Addison, Texas. I also obtained my Private Pilot Single-Engine Land Pilot's license while at Sabre.

Eventually, the expense and the income of the company did not balance, so payroll for me and my staff became intermittent. I went on to

Office and Personnel Manager for and oil and gas consulting company in Dallas.

While with Purvin & Gertz, Inc. Oil & Gas Consultants, I began to be more aware of how quickly the use of computers was expanding from just engineering to the business world. Since I had received considerable bonuses at Purvin & Gertz, I chose to actually go back to the University of North Texas full-time and obtain a Master of Business Administration (MBA) degree with a specialty addition of Business Computer Information Systems.

My first and only job after graduation was with a Fort Worth, Texas, defense contractor then known as General Dynamics. They manufactured fighter and bomber aircraft for many air forces throughout the world. It was an amazing experience as a computer programmer and then a systems analyst.

Printed in the United States
by Baker & Taylor Publisher Services